Oscar Niemeyer

Casa das Canoas
Casa Cavanelas

Residential Masterpieces 28
Oscar Niemeyer
Casa das Canoas
Casa Cavanelas

Photographs, text and edited by Yoshio Futagawa
Art direction: Gan Hosoya

Copyright © 2019 A.D.A. EDITA Tokyo Co., Ltd.
3-12-14 Sendagaya, Shibuya-ku, Tokyo 151-0051, Japan
All rights reserved. No part of this publication may be reproduced,
stored in a retrieval system, or transmitted,
in any form or by any means, electronic, mechanical,
photocopying, recording, or otherwise,
without permission in writing from the publisher.

Copyright of drawings
©2019 Oscar Niemeyer Foundation
Copyright of photographs
©2019 GA photographers

Printed and bound in Japan

ISBN 978-4-87140-561-4 C1352

Residential Masterpieces 28

Oscar Niemeyer
Casa das Canoas
Rio de Janeiro, Brazil, 1950-53
Casa Cavanelas
Rio de Janeiro, Brazil, 1954

Text and Photographed by Yoshio Futagawa

世界現代住宅全集28
オスカー・ニーマイヤー
カノアスの家
ブラジル，リオデジャネイロ　1950-53
カヴァネラス邸
ブラジル，リオデジャネイロ　1954

撮影・文・編集：二川由夫

オスカー・ニーマイヤー，超越者の住まい──二川由夫
Homes by a Transcender *by Yoshio Futagawa*

建築家オスカー・ニーマイヤーは，その超越的な創造力を以て20世紀の近代建築黎明期から21世紀までを駆け抜けた数少ない巨匠の一人であった。自国ブラジルはもとより，一時活動の場を移したヨーロッパに多くの名作建築を残している。その多くは公共建築であり，彼の唯一無比の圧倒的な造形力と，その背後にある，利用者である市民に対して構想された大胆かつ緻密な建築計画によって，新しい市民空間の可能性と，新しい建築が社会に対して振る舞うイコンとしての有り様を提示した。

例えばサンパウロの「イビラプエラ公園」(1951-54年) に架けられた大屋根は，単に雲形のフォルムにみる美しさだけでなく，その下に生まれる市民の憩いの場がこの公園を特別なものにし，また，大胆で美しいシルエットを纏う美術館やホールはその街の強いイコンとなって求心力を生み出す。首都ブラジリアの都市計画では，ブラジルという新世界国家の他に無い進取の精神を世界に示した。ニーマイヤーの残した名作に影響を受けたフォロワーは世界中に多く居れども，彼の超越的な独自性を乗り越えた者は未だに出現しないような，孤高の巨匠建築家であった。

104年の生涯を通して多くの公共建築を手がけたニーマイヤーは，住宅建築もまた手がけている。戦前に実現した一連の住宅は，師匠であるル・コルビュジエの影響が大きく表れたモダニズムの「白い住宅」を設計しているが，やがてブラジルの風土や文化の影響の下，ヨーロッパ由来のモダニズム建築の理念はローカライズされ，自身の卓越したデザイン力を表出させた住宅を手がけることになった。しかしながら公共建築の持つヒロイックな力強さや祝祭性，大鉈を振るうような造形の誇示（それらは決してエゴイスティックな空回りをするようなものでなく，万民を感動させる程の力量が裏付けにあるわけだが）とは違う方向性が住宅建築には与えられていることは興味深い。ニーマイヤーの住宅建築の多くが描く建築的なテーマは，パーソナルな空間の創出であり，社会と隔絶された，クライアントにとっての「特別な場」であった。

ここに取り上げられた2軒の住宅，「カノアスの家」(1950-53年) と「カヴァネラス邸」(1954年) は共に1950年代に建てられた住宅であるが，2軒の家のコントラストはとても興味深いものである。「カノアスの家」はニーマイヤー自身の家であり，建築家がプライベートに求めた空間の真実が見てとれ，一方の「カヴァネラス邸」ではランドスケープデザイナー，ロベルト・

Architect Oscar Niemeyer is one of the few masters who, with his transcendental creativity, dashed from the dawn of 20th-century modern architecture into the 21st century. He left a number of masterpieces not only in his home country Brazil but also in Europe where he temporarily relocated his office. Many of them being public buildings, they became icons that demonstrated potentials of new civic spaces and behaviors of new architecture against society, through his truly unique, breathtaking forms and audacious yet elaborate architectural planning conceived for the citizens who are the users that can be found behind such forms.

For example, the grand roof over the Ibirapuera Park (1951-54) in São Paulo creates, besides the beauty of its cloud-shaped form, areas of refuge for the citizens that make this park a special place. Auditorium and museums clad in bold, stunning silhouettes are powerful icons of the city that generate an unifying force. Through the urban planning for the capital Brasília he showed to the world the unparalleled progressive spirit of Brazil, a nation of the New World. Many followers around the world were influenced by his works, but none has yet surmounted his transcendental originality, making him a master architect who stood apart.

Niemeyer who, through his 104-year-long life, frequently worked on public architectures, also designed residential architectures. While the series of houses realized before the war are 'white houses' that show significant influence from his mentor Le Corbusier, in the course of time, the principles of Modernist architecture of European origin came to be localized, affected by Brazilian climate and culture, that pushed him to create houses that manifest remarkable design abilities of his own. However, it is interesting that his residential architectures are not oriented toward showing off heroic might and festivity of public architecture or authority-exercising forms (in spite of being supported by his competence to impress the whole nation without running around in egoistic circles, that is). Architectural themes observed among many of Niemeyer's residential buildings often involved creation of personal space—a 'special place' for the client that is isolated from the society.

Two houses featured in this volume, Das Canoas House (1950-53) and Cavanelas Residence (1954), were both built in the 1950s. The contrast between them is quite intriguing: Das Canoas House, being Niemeyer's own residence, demonstrates the spatial truth in privacy that the architect has explored;

ブーレ・マルクスとの協働によってつくり出された華やかな演出に驚かされる。

「カノアスの家」
リオデジャネイロの世界的な観光名所，コパカバーナのビーチから車で西に30分ほど行ったジャングルの中に建築家の自邸は建てられた。敷地は濃厚な深い緑に囲まれ，聳え立つ山を見上げ，遠くに大西洋を見渡す，プライバシーを十分確保した静かな土地である。ニーマイヤーは敷地内にあった最も特徴的なエレメントである巨石に着目し，これに錨をおろすかのごとくこの地に住宅を建てた。敷地を北側からの斜路によってアプローチすると，木々の間に特徴的なフォルムの白い屋根と水色のプールが岩と共に現れる。岩を介して向き合うように配置される白い屋根と水色のプールは，共に自由な曲線に縁取られた双子の関係にあり，岩は内外の空間を結びつける重要な役目を与えられて二つのエレメントを結んでいる。

屋根のコンクリート・スラブは大理石のリムに縁取られた継ぎ目のない白いプレーンな面であり，敷地の緑の密度を尊重するかのようにその高さを抑えられて，8本の鉄柱と北側のオペークの壁面に支えられ，その下に内外の場所をつくり出している。この屋根の下，リオの強い陽射しを避けるように奥まって配置されたガラスとオペークの壁面は屋根とは異なるフォルムの平面形をつくり出している。

1階は西側の台所以外は仕切りの無い一室空間であり，居間と食堂に使われる。北側のガラス壁は玄関となるスライド扉が与えられ，北側方向に張り出した屋根の下に半屋外の居間となるエリアと繋げられている。このガラス壁は前述の岩の上を跨ぐように西側の台所へカーブを描きながら続いている。南側にもガラス壁が与えられて，スライド扉によって外部へアクセスでき，居間・食堂からは大西洋を見ることができる。居間を囲むように配置された北側，オペークの壁面は，南北に2枚のガラス壁で外部と視覚的に繋げられた中央の空間とは異なる閉じたもので，それらは仕切りがないためグラデーションで性格の変わる連続した一室空間となっている。外部の壁は緑色に塗られ，その内部は木製，温かみを演出している。また食堂背後の，丸テーブルに呼応するように湾曲した壁面も同様の木製仕上げが与えられている。食堂の背後にある洗面室はスカイライトが

Cavanelas Residence on the other hand, startles with spectacular features orchestrated through his collaboration with landscape designer Roberto Burle Marx.

Das Canoas House
A 30-minute drive west from the beach of Copacabana, Rio de Janeiro's world-famous tourist attraction, it was in a jungle that the architect built his own residence. Enclosed in lush deep green, the site sits in a quiet location on the side of a soaring hill with a distant view over the Atlantic where privacy is carefully maintained. Niemeyer focused on a giant rock, the most prominent element found on the site, and built his home as if anchoring the house to this rock. As one approaches the site via a ramp from the north, the white roof with a characteristic form and the light-blue pool emerge from the trees along with the rock. With the rock standing in between, the white roof and the light-blue pool face each other like twins that are both framed by free-flowing curves. The rock plays an important role of associating the inside with the outside as it connects the two elements.

A seam-free, plain, white surface rimmed with marble, the concrete slab of the roof is given a limited height as if respecting the density of the site's vegetation, supported on 8 steel pillars and an opaque wall on the north side as it creates interior and exterior spaces underneath. Under this roof, the glazed and opaque wall surfaces set back to avoid the intense sunlight of Rio de Janeiro draw a floor plan that do not match the roof's form.

The main floor is, except for the kitchen on the west, an open-plan space accommodating the living and dining rooms. A sliding door serving as the entrance is installed in the glass wall on the north side, and opens to the semi-outdoor lounge area topped by a roof that protrudes northward. This glass wall almost strides over the rock and extends to the kitchen on the west, drawing a curve. Another glass wall stands on the south side, with a sliding door that offers outside access and a view over the Atlantic from the living/dining rooms. The opaque wall on the north surrounds the living room, the latter being an enclosed type of area unlike the one in the center between two glass walls on north and south with visual connection to the outside. Since the two areas are not partitioned, the entire space is a continuous open plan featuring a seamless change of spatial character. Painted green on the outside, the wall is covered with wood on the inside for a touch of warmth. Another

与えられた小さいながら明るい空間である。
　西端の階段は石の横を地下階へと下がって行き，あたかも岩の洞窟に入って行くような演出がされている。地下階はプライベートなサロンを中心に置き，その南北に寝室と付随する浴室が機能的に配置されている。地下階は敷地の高低差を利用して設けられているため，その南側に配置された三つの寝室には窓が設けられ，また，サロンや浴室にも連続する丸窓のハイサイドライトが設けられ，自然光を導いている。
　「カノアスの家」は，彫刻的な美意識を湛えた建築が，自然と造作された庭のコンテクストに対して溶け込み過ぎず，主張し過ぎずといった絶妙のバランスで成立している。華美な材料や，先鋭的な建築操作が空間を特殊なものにすることなく，建築家の求めた，豊かな自然の受容された平穏な暮らしがそこにある。周囲の自然や庭の様相はこの住空間を成立させる最も重要なエレメントであり，言い換えれば，この環境全体が住宅そのものである。

「カヴァネラス邸」
　ニーマイヤーは，コルビュジエに見出されるきっかけとなったルシオ・コスタの主導による「教育保健省」(1937-43年)のプロジェクトで，同世代のランドスケープデザイナー，ロベルト・ブーレ・マルクスと出会い，その後，多くのプロジェクトで協働することとなった。前出，「カノアスの家」も2人の協働であった。「カノアスの家」でのランドスケープデザインが自然環境の延長線上にあるような調整的な仕事であったのに対して，「カヴァネラス邸」では幾何学的，絵画的なデザインがなされている。「カヴァネラス邸」において，ニーマイヤーはこの大胆なランドスケープを最大限に生かす住宅建築をつくっている。
　敷地は風景の豊かな丘陵地の中にあり，整地された平坦な土地で，約7,000平米の広さを持つ。周囲の雄大で美しい山々や自然のつくり出す景色を借景にし，敷地にはブーレ・マルクスの手による庭が全面的に広がる。ニーマイヤーの手掛けた住宅建築は，この庭を見渡す敷地中央に配置されている。
　住宅は南北に長い長方形のプランで，その4隅に設けられた4本の壁

wall behind the dining room with a curve responding to the round table is given a similar wooden finish. The washroom behind the dining room is a small but bright space lit by a skylight.

On the western end is a staircase leading down to the basement floor past the rock that gives an impression of entering a cave. This floor consists of a private salon in the center and bedrooms on north and south with ensuite bathrooms arranged in a functional manner. Since the layout of the basement floor takes advantage of the level difference of the terrain, natural light is available: each of the three bedrooms arranged on the south side is equipped with a window; the salon as well as bathrooms are lit through a series of round high side lights.

Das Canoas House is based on the perfect balance that an architecture filled with sculpturesque aesthetics manages to maintain, avoiding too much integration and too much advocacy against the contexts of both landscaped garden and nature. What can be found there is a tranquil living in which nature's bounty is accepted that the architect has wanted, without ornate materials nor aggressive architectural manipulations that turn the spaces into something peculiar. The surrounding nature and various aspects of the garden are the most important elements that make up this residential space—in other words, this entire environment is the house itself.

Cavanelas Residence

Niemeyer met Roberto Burle Marx, a landscape designer of the same generation, with whom he later came to collaborate on a number of projects, through the project for the Ministry of Education and Health (1937-43) lead by Lúcio Costa which gave him the chance to be spotted by Le Corbusier. Das Canoas House presented earlier was also a fruit of their collaboration. Whereas in Das Canoas House the landscape design involved an adjustment type of work found along the line of natural environment, in Cavanelas Residence landscape design is geometric and picturesque. With Cavanelas Residence, Niemeyer created a residential architecture by taking full advantage of this audacious landscaping.

Located among scenic rolling hills, the site is on a flat, leveled ground with an area of approximately 7,000 m². With the imposing, beautiful mountains and surrounding natural scenery as a backdrop, the garden by Burle Marx occupies the full extent of the site while the residential building by Niemeyer stands at the center of the site with a panoramic view over the

柱に張り渡された天幕のような軽快な形の大屋根が架かるシンプルな構成だが，これは意匠的なもので，実際の構造はこれら4本の柱に加え，間に立てられた2枚の壁が梁を支えている。4本の壁柱は3角形の立面を持ち，あたかも屋根を引っ張り上げているかのような逆カテナリー形式の力学的なジェスチャーが与えられている。この力学的ジェスチャーはニーマイヤーがここで表現したい造形の意思であり，実際の構造との矛盾は，このフォルムと庭／環境との対話が生み出す物語の強度によって吹き飛んでしまっている。ニーマイヤーによる大胆な構造的フォルムを持つ一連の建築においてよくあることでもあり，構造的なシルエットは必ずしも力学的な理由によらない。この住宅は簡易な天幕のパヴィリオンという役回りを与えられ，周囲の庭との関係はより強固なものになっている。

　大屋根の下，陽射しから逃れ，さらに半屋外のテラス空間をもたらすように南北2枚の石張りの壁面と，東西2枚のガラスの多い壁面は，それぞれ屋根の縁より内側に後退して配置され，主空間である居間と食堂を形成している。南側壁面中央には暖炉が配置される。反対の北側壁面は東側に突き出され，背後に隠すように配置された台所や三つの寝室に十分なプライバシーを確保している。

　庭は大胆な図案が植栽によって形づくられている。建物の西側は流れるような図案がカラフルな植栽によって池に向かって描かれる。これに対して建物の東側の庭は，種類の違う植栽によって整然と描かれたチェッカーフラッグ柄が敷き詰められ，フォーマルな性格が与えられている。東側の庭にはプールが配置され，居間・食堂の正面には彫像が焦点となるように置かれている。

　図案は抽象絵画的で，ブーレ・マルクスが手がけた一連の仕事に共通するクオリティを持ったものであり，この超自然的な庭は，自然と庭が見事に統合的に完成された祝祭的な「ハレの空間」であり，この住宅建築はこの庭を楽しむためのもの，という明快な意思の結晶であり，ニーマイヤーのブーレ・マルクスの仕事に対する尊敬の念と協働の喜びに溢れている。

entire garden.

The house has a rectangular plan along the north-south axis and a simple composition involving four wall pillars standing on its four corners and a large, airy roof spanning across them like an awning which is in fact just a design feature—the real structure consists of these four pillars and two additional walls installed in between that support the beam. The four wall pillars have a triangular elevation and are given a reverse catenary-type of dynamic gesture as if they are pulling up the roof. This dynamic gesture is like an intention of the form that Neimeyer wishes to express here; contradiction between the appearance and the actual structure is eventually blown away by the intensity of the story generated by the dialogue between this form and the garden/environment. It is nothing unusual among Niemeyer's other architectures with bold structural forms, as structural silhouettes are not necessarily consequences of dynamics. The house plays a role of a simple pavilion made out of an awning, and keeps a reinforced relationship with the surrounding garden.

Under the main roof, away from the sunshine and so as to create a semi-outdoor terrace space, two stone-clad walls on south and north and two others that are heavily glazed on east and west are set back from the roof edge to accommodate the living and dining rooms that constitute the main space. At the center of the southern wall is installed a fireplace. Northern wall on the opposite side protrudes to the east to ensure privacy to the kitchen and three bedrooms that are hidden behind.

In the garden, planting draws a bold pattern. On the western side of the building is a flowing pattern realized with colorful plants that stretches toward the pond. On the other hand the garden on the eastern side of the building is covered with orderly-drawn checker-board pattern using several types of plants, and is given a formal character. A swimming pool is also installed in the eastern garden. Facing the living/dining rooms is a sculpture that is placed as a point of focus.

The pattern looks like abstract art with quality that matches other works by Burle Marx. This supernatural garden is a festive 'space of *hale* (sacredness)' where nature and garden are successfully integrated to perfection. Here, residential architecture is the embodiment of a clear and simple will to enjoy the garden, brimming with Niemeyer's respect for Burle Marx's work as well as pleasure in collaborating with him.

English translation by Lisa Tani

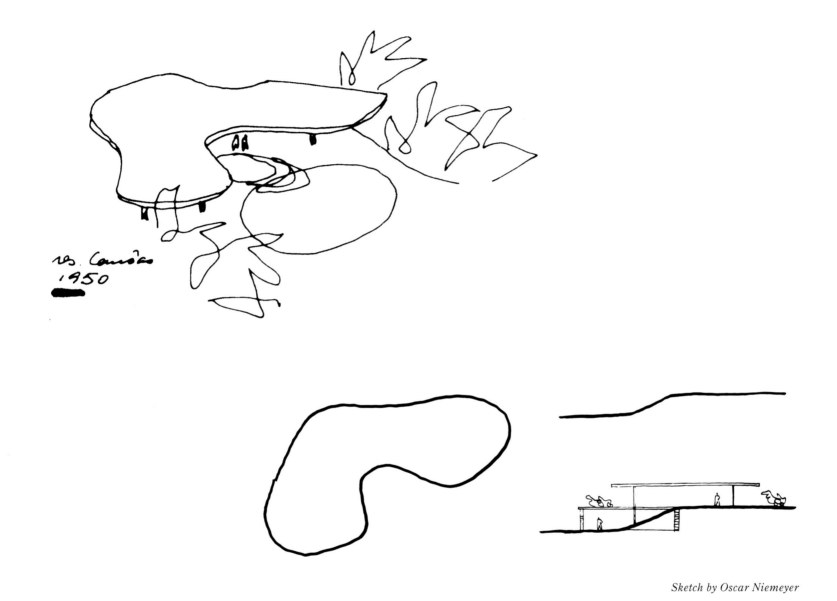

Sketch by Oscar Niemeyer

Casa das Canoas 1950-53

View from approach on north

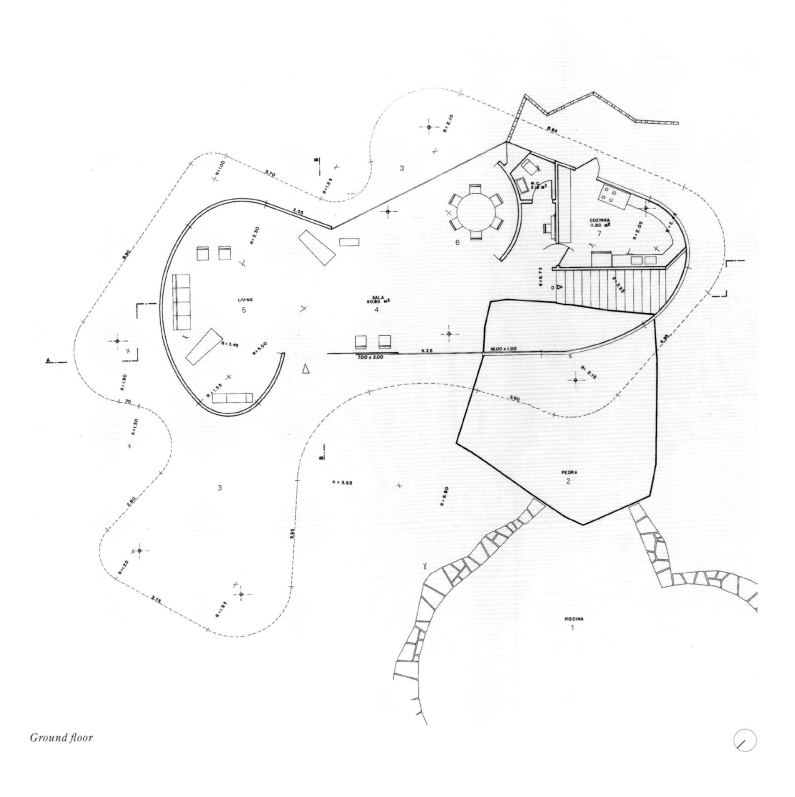

Ground floor

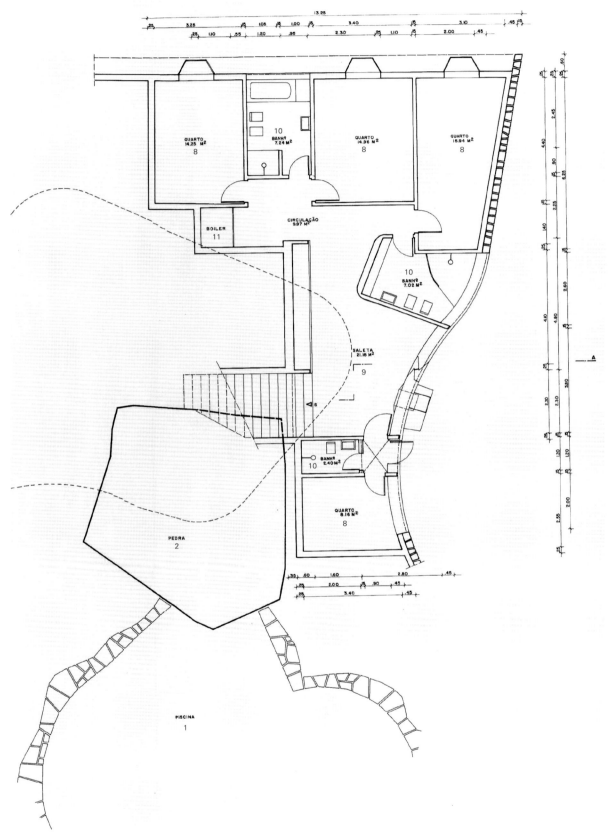

Basement

1 SWIMMING POOL
2 STONE
3 PATIO
4 HALL
5 LIVING ROOM
6 DINING ROOM
7 KITCHEN
8 BEDROOM
9 SALON
10 BATHROOM
11 BOILER ROOM

Overall view from front court

Swimming pool and patio

View from patio. Stone between house and swimming pool

Stone and roof

View toward entrance

View toward patio and approach

Hall

View from hall

Boundary wall over stone

Dining room

Living room

View through window of living room

Staircase to basement

Staircase with stone

Salon at basement. Chair designed by Oscar Niemeyer

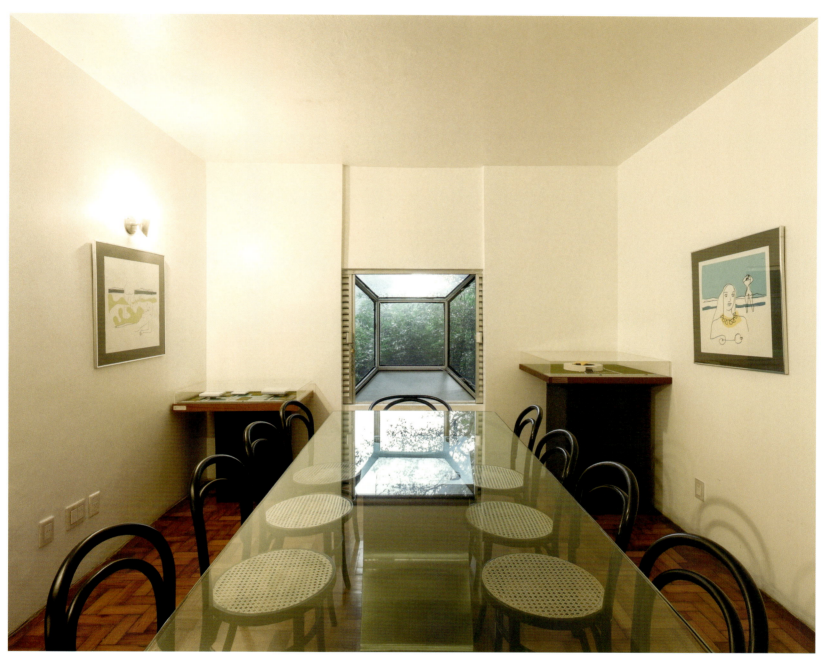

Room originally used as bedroom

Poping out window of bedroom

Bathroom on ground floor   *Bathroom on basement*

Patio on south

View toward South Atlantic Ocean over roof

Casa Cavanelas 1954

Distant view over pond from west

Approach

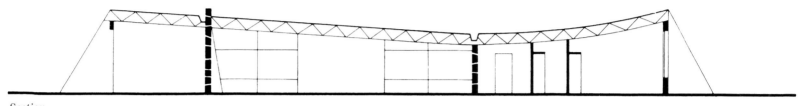

Section

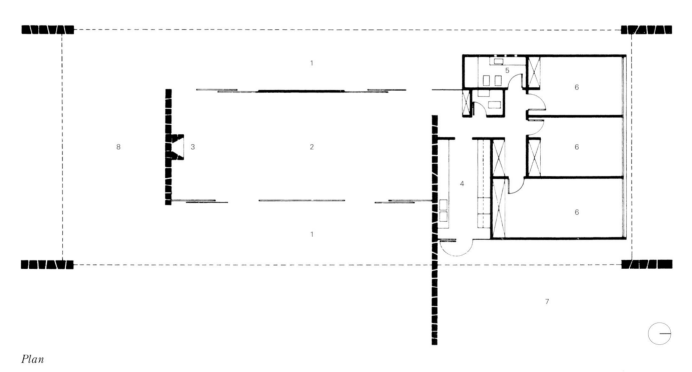

Plan

1 PATIO
2 LIVING/DINING ROOM
3 FIREPLACE
4 KITCHEN
5 BATHROOM
6 BEDROOM
7 SERVICE COURT
8 GARAGE

View from approach. House and landscape by Roberto Burle Marx appears below

West elevation

View from east. Checkered flag pattern of lawn and plants.

View from east over swimming pool

Garden on east

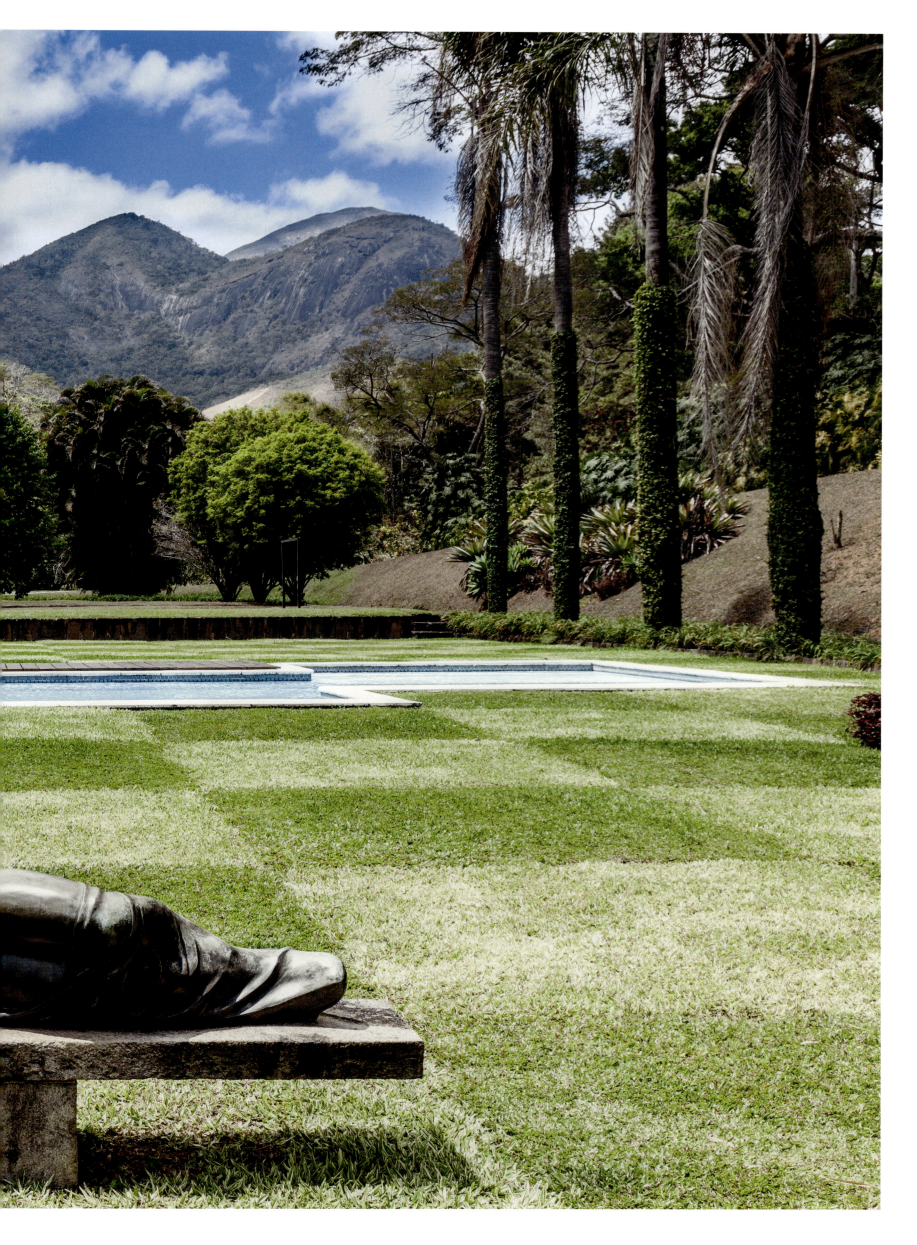

View from roof of fiber cement panel toward garden

Triangular wall column supporting at four corners

View from south. Landscape with checkered pattern on east (right), curvilinear on west (left)

Patio on west

Patio on east

Living room

Corridor. Kitchen on left

Living/dining room. View toward east garden

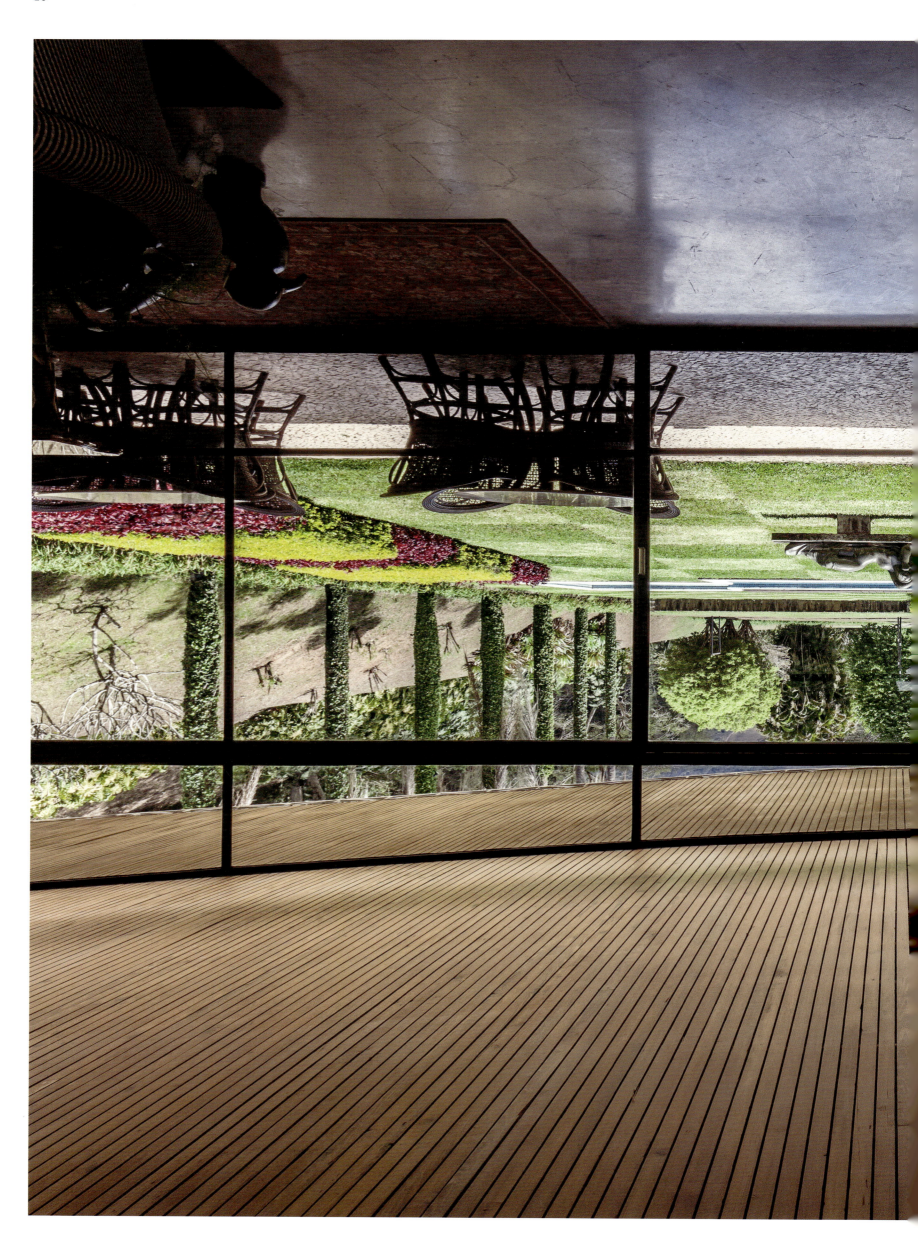

Garden, looking toward west

Photographs are taken by Yoshio Futagawa except as noted below.
Cover, pp.14-17, p.20, pp.24-27, p.30, p.31 middle, p.33, p.35, p.36, p.37 right: photos by Yukio Futagawa

世界現代住宅全集 28

オスカー・ニーマイヤー
カノアスの家
カサ・ダス・カノアス

2019年4月25日発行
編纂・文・構成：二川由夫
アート・ディレクション：鈴谷巌
印刷・製本：大日本印刷株式会社
制作・発行：エーディーエー・エディタ・トーキョー
151-0051　東京都渋谷区千駄ヶ谷 3-12-14
TEL. (03) 3403-1381 (代)

落丁本乱丁本はお取替致します

ISBN 978-4-87140-561-4 C1352